THE VALUE OF UNDERSTANDING

The Story of Margaret Mead

VALUE COMMUNICATIONS, INC.
PUBLISHERS
LA JOLLA, CALIFORNIA

ILLUSTRATED BY

THE VALUE OF UNDERSTANDING

The Story of
Margaret Mead

BY SPENCER JOHNSON, M.D.

First Edition
Manufactured in the United States of America
For information write to: ValueTales, P.O. Box 1012
La Jolla, CA 92038

Library of Congress Cataloging in Publication Data

Johnson, Spencer.
    The value of understanding.

    (ValueTales series)
    SUMMARY: A biography, stressing the understanding and tolerance, of an anthropologist who did extensive studies of primitive cultures.
    [1.   Mead, Margaret, 1901–1978
2.   Anthropologists.   3.   Prejudices]   1.   Mead, Margaret.
1901–1978   —Juvenile literature.   2.   Anthropologists—
United States—Biography—Juvenile literature.   I.   Title.
GN21.M36J63   301.2′092′4   [B] [92]   79-9800

ISBN 0-916392-37-6

This tale is about a woman who tried to understand people, Margaret Mead. The story that follows is based on events in her life. More historical facts about Margaret Mead can be found on page 63.

Once upon a time...

not so very long ago, a little girl named Margaret Mead lived in Pennsylvania with her mother, father, and grandmother.

In many ways Margaret's family was much like other families, but in many ways it was different.

Margaret's father was a college professor, and when she was very small Margaret didn't know exactly what that meant. "What is a professor, Daddy" she asked one day, "and why are *you* one?"

"A professor is someone who keeps on learning," said her father, "and who teaches people what he knows. I do this because I can think of nothing more important for someone to do than to add to the world's knowledge."

"Perhaps when I grow up," said Margaret to her father, "I can add to the world's knowledge, too."

Margaret's mother was a college graduate at a time when not very many women went to college. She was a social scientist who cared very much about other people.

Margaret's grandmother lived with them too. She had been a teacher, a school principal, and a wife and mother. Now she was also a loving grandmother.

Margaret loved her mother and her father and her grandmother. She was glad to be part of such a wonderful family.

When Margaret was very young, she thought that all grown-up women were probably a lot like her mother and grandmother— that they studied and read books and cared about what happened in the world, and that they talked about their thoughts and ideas.

But then, when Margaret was about ten years old, her mother took her to a parade. It wasn't the usual sort of parade, with brass bands and marching men. It was a parade of many women who marched down the street and handed out pieces of paper to the people who crowded along the curbs.

"Why are we doing this?" Margaret asked her mother.

"Because we're suffragettes," said her mother. "We're trying to get suffrage—the right to vote—for women, just like the men already have."

"You mean women don't have the right to vote?" cried Margaret. "But that's not fair!"

"Of course it's not fair," said her mother, "but most people don't understand that yet."

One day not long after that, Margaret noticed that her mother was watching her and writing things down in a notebook.

"What are you doing, Mother?" Margaret asked.

"I'm thinking about you and writing about what you do," said Mrs. Mead. "I like to notice people and try to understand why they are the way they are. And after all, you're one of the most important people in the world to me!"

Margaret felt very proud to be a part of her mother's notebook. She liked it that her mother paid so much attention to her. Sometimes she tried to explain to other children in the neighborhood how she felt, but they didn't seem to understand. Neither did her younger brother or sisters. They were too small.

So, in time, Margaret learned to just think these thoughts to herself when she was alone. "When I grow up, I'll keep notebooks, too," she decided. "I wonder what else I'll do when I grow up."

Of course no one could tell Margaret what she would do. So she thought and thought, and puzzled and wondered, and she became more and more confused. Finally, an amazing thing happened!

A little figure seemed to pop out of the air, and appeared, as if by magic, right in front of Margaret. "Well, you could be a social scientist like your mother," said a tiny voice, "or a teacher, like Grandma. Or maybe you could do something completely different!"

"This isn't really happening," said Margaret. "I'm talking to myself. That's what I'm doing. And I'm listening to my own ideas. What a wonderful way to do it," she thought.

"I'm Per," the tiny figure said, introducing itself to Margaret.

"Per? Is that your full name?" Margaret asked politely.

"No, my last name is Sun, so I'm really Per Sun."

Margaret laughed and laughed. "What a great name!" she said. "Are you a boy or a girl?"

"That really isn't terribly important, is it?" said Per Sun. "You know what your mother always says, 'We're all just persons.'"

"What *is* important, though, is not to worry so much about what you'll do when you grow up," said Per Sun. "You know that you want to understand people like your mother does, and that you want to add to the world's knowledge like your father does. If you really want to do those two things, you'll succeed in doing them. You'll find out *how* to do them when the time is right—when you are ready. Believe me."

Because they were Margaret's own thoughts, Margaret did believe. Of course as she grew up she kept on thinking about what she would do. She went to college in New York, just as her mother and grandmother had done. Per Sun went with her, for she still liked the company of her own thoughts.

16

"Perhaps I should study art," she said to Per Sun one day as she walked across the campus. "Or maybe politics or science would be better."

"When you find the right thing, you'll know," counseled Per Sun. "But now you'd better hurry or you'll be late for your new class!"

Margaret began to run. Per Sun skipped after her, and when they reached the class, the professor was there, ready to begin the lecture.

"My name is Franz Boas," he said, "and our subject is anthropology. That is the scientific study of people."

"A study of people!" whispered Margaret to Per Sun. "It sounds wonderful."

The professor went on with his lecture. "Anthropologists are scientists who try to understand persons from all over the world and from every time," he said. "An anthropologist tries to think of all people as if they were members of one very large family."

"I think I know what he means," said Margaret. "He means that every person is a part of the human family."

Per smiled. At last Margaret had found what she wanted to do. Margaret Mead wanted to be an anthropologist.

Margaret studied anthropology for several years. Then she got a job at the American Museum of Natural History in New York City. At last she was ready to begin her life's work.

In those days, most anthropologists studied ancient civilizations. They read old books and they searched through ruined cities for things that would help them figure out how people lived many years ago.

Margaret Mead did not want to search through ruins or to read ancient books. She thought she had a better way to find out about the human family.

Can you guess what it was?

"I'll find a civilization that's a long way from New York," she decided. "I'll go there and see for myself how the people there live today."

"If you aren't afraid to live in a strange place, among people who have different customs, that might be a wonderful way to work," said Professor Boaz. "Perhaps you could find the answer to a very important question: Do all boys and girls, no matter where they live, find it difficult to grow up into happy adults?"

Margaret thought she would very much like to know the answer to that question, and she decided to go live among the people of Samoa, a group of islands far away in the South Seas. She hurried home to tell her mother and father, her grandmother, and her brother and sisters.

"You'll miss the comfort and love you always find at home," said Per Sun.

"Yes, I will," said Margaret, "but think what a great adventure I'll be having!"

Margaret hugged each member of her family. Then she went off.

Her father smiled. He could see that Margaret was doing exactly what she wanted to do. "She never looked back," he said.

"What do you think we'll find when we get to Samoa?" said Per Sun, once they were on their way.

Margaret laughed. "A long time ago you told me I'd have to wait to find out what I wanted to do. Now we have to wait and see what Samoa will be like. We can't know until we get there, can we?"

"Of course not," Per Sun agreed. "Just the same, I can't help wondering what it will be like on an island where the people have a different language and different customs."

When Margaret Mead landed in Samoa, she decided that she would live in the village of Viatogi. However, the native chief there was suspicious. "Who are you and why have you come here?" he asked.

"I am called Margaret Mead," she told him. "I have come many, many miles to see you. My people would like to know more about your people and your ways. With your kind permission, I would like to live among you so that I can tell your story truly."

The chief was still suspicious. "You came only so that you can tell our story truly?" he said. "Why is it so important for you to do this?"

"Because if my people can understand people here," said Margaret, "perhaps we will be better able to understand ourselves."

"That is a wise answer," said the chief, and he invited Margaret to stay and eat with his family.

Margaret soon learned that in Samoa people ate food with their fingers. So she did too.

"People would think I was rude if I did this at home," she said. "But here they would think I was rude if I didn't. In Samoa I should not criticize the way people eat—or the way they live, either."

"Indeed, you should not," whispered Per Sun. "If you really want to understand someone, there is no better way than to live for a while as they do."

Soon Margaret was not only eating as the Samoans ate, she was also learning to speak as they spoke.

"The people seem very pleased when I can understand what they're talking about," she said.

"They're so pleased that I think they are going to do something special for you," said Per Sun.

Can you guess what that special thing was?

The people were building a house so that Margaret could live in a home of her own while she was in Samoa.

"What a wonderful surprise!" said Margaret. "But I would be very pleased if you would build my house so that it has a roof but no walls."

"No walls?" echoed Per Sun. "Why on earth do you want a house without walls?"

"So that I can see and hear everything that goes on around me," said Margaret. "To understand the Samoan people I must see for myself how they live."

So Margaret's house was built with no walls, and she could sit in it and see the Samoan children at play. Sometimes she took photographs of the youngsters with the camera she had brought from America.

"They have fun playing, don't they?" said Per Sun.

"Haven't you noticed?" said Margaret. "They do more than just play!"

"You are right," said Per Sun. "These children work as well as play."

Margaret saw that children as young as six years old were taught to feed their little brothers and sisters and to take care of them. At first the mother stayed nearby as the older child went about this task, but eventually the children learned to take care of one another all by themselves.

The Samoan girls learned to weave cloth, too. By the time a girl was nine years old, she could make clothes for her family, and she could cook meals and serve them. By the time a Samoan girl was thirteen, she could take full care of a family.

One day Margaret noticed that a certain young man was paying special attention to a girl named Namu.

The young man was named Alo, and he was just about ready to choose a wife.

Like most Samoan boys, he had learned how to manage a canoe. He could fish for bonito and he could catch eels. He could plant taro and coconut trees. He had learned all of these things before he was fifteen years old.

32

The children of Samoa became Margaret's "notebook children," just as she had been her mother's notebook child. "They spend part of each day playing," Margaret wrote in her notebook, "and they spend part of every day working, too."

Not only did Margaret write in her notebook about the Samoan youngsters, she also loved to write letters home to her grandmother. And after she had been on the island for a while, she wrote about a special ceremony she had attended for Namu and Alo.

What sort of ceremony do you think it was?

It was a wedding ceremony!

Alo and Namu were very, very happy. Their parents were pleased, too. The young couple liked each other very much, and they were well prepared to take care of each other.

After nine months, Margaret Mead knew that she had the answer to Professor Boas' question. ''All boys and girls do not find it difficult to grow up into happy adults,'' she told Per Sun. ''For some children, growing up is hard. But in Samoa it is easy.''

Per Sun nodded in agreement. "It *is* easy. At least, it's easier than growing up in America!"

But Margaret wanted to make certain that she had the right answer, so she talked to many other Samoan people. Each one said the same thing. Growing up in Samoa was not difficult.

One day, when Margaret was alone for a moment, Per Sun said, "Everyone in the village likes to talk with you."

"I know," said Margaret. "Isn't it nice? The Samoan people are so courteous."

"Yes, they are," said Per Sun, "but that isn't the only reason. They enjoy being with you. You make each one feel important because you listen carefully. They know that you really want to understand what they believe in and how they think.

"You laugh with them, too, and you make them laugh. They like that. Anyone would."

It made Margaret happy to hear this, and she felt good as she continued with her work—watching and taking notes and snapping pictures of the people. And when at last it was time for Margaret to return home, the Samoans had grown to love her. Many of them hugged her goodbye.

"This has been an interesting time," Margaret whispered to Per Sun, "but I can hardly wait to get home and see my own family."

There was great excitement when Margaret finally arrived home. "Tell us everything!" cried her sisters. "Absolutely everything!" ordered her brother.

So Margaret told how she had sat cross-legged on the ground to eat with her fingers. She told about how the food was cooked over pits of stone and served on palm leaves. She told about her house with no walls, and about the wedding of Namu and Alo.

As Margaret described her experiences in detail, each person in the Mead family could almost feel what it was like to be in Samoa. "Your experiences could be made into a wonderful book," her family assured her.

And that's exactly what Margaret did next. She studied the notes she had made in Samoa. Then she set to work writing her book. It was called *Coming of Age in Samoa*, and it described the way youngsters were raised in the islands, and how happily they grew up.

Margaret Mead was only twenty-six years old when she wrote this book. She found that writing was hard work, but she wanted very much to do it. She wanted people to understand the customs of Samoa.

Many people read Margaret's book after it was published.

"What an exciting book," said some. "It's like reading an adventure story. I can almost feel what it's like to be in Samoa. In fact, I think I know what it's like to be Samoan."

Anthropologists who read the book could now see the value of what Margaret had done. She had "gone into the field" herself. That is, she had gone to where the people lived so that she could better understand them. Soon other anthropologists began to do the same thing.

More and more, people began to see that there could be more than one way of doing things. People began to understand and accept the differences among people.

But Margaret was so busy that she wasn't really aware of the excitement her book was causing.

Can you guess what she was doing?

She was traveling to another new land! Once again it was far from her home.

"Why are we taking *this* trip, Margaret?" Per Sun asked. "I should think you'd had enough of being away from your family. Won't you miss your mother and father, and Grandma, and your brother and sisters?"

"Of course I'll miss them," said Margaret, "but I still have so much to learn. I want to understand more about why people are the way they are."

"That's a big order," said Per. "It's a good thing you have so much energy."

"I suppose it is," said Margaret, "I can't help wondering whether we are the way we are because we're born that way or whether we are shaped and molded by the way we're raised. Perhaps if I study another group of children who are not raised like American children, and if I see what kind of adults they become, I can begin to learn the answer."

After a long voyage, Margaret Mead and Per Sun landed on the primitive island of Manus. This island was in the Admiralty group, north of New Guinea. Margaret was six thousand miles from home.

"It isn't a lot like New York, is it?" said Per Sun. "It isn't like Samoa, either."

As usual, Per Sun was right. The people of the Manus tribe lived in thatched huts that were set on stilts above the green water of a wide lagoon. They were tall, and their skin was brown. The men wore loincloths and tied their hair up in knots. The women wore grass skirts and shaved their heads.

And the children? They were also very different from the children in Samoa. Can you guess *how* they were different?

45

They did not do any work at all. They did nothing but play from morning till night. They romped in the water until they were tired. Then they rested. Then they played again.

Even the older children were given no responsibilities. If they didn't want to do a thing, they simply didn't do it.

"My word!" cried Per Sun. "What kind of adults will they be when they grow up?"

"That's what we came to find out," said Margaret, and she looked around at the adults in the Manus tribe. And what did she see?

She saw people who were unhappy and angry. The young men were not allowed to choose the girls they wanted to marry. The choice was made for them by their parents. And the parents of a boy had to pay a great deal of money to the parents of a girl so that the boy could marry her.

After the wedding, the boy was heavily in debt, for he had to repay his father for the money spent on his bride. Most boys felt trapped and resentful, and since neither boys nor girls had been taught to take care of one another, the couples were often dreadfully unhappy.

"Golly!" said Per Sun. "Growing up in Manus is a lot different from growing up in Samoa. It might look like fun at first, but it doesn't turn out too well."

"No, it doesn't, does it?" said Margaret thoughtfully. "Can you imagine how unhappy our young friends Namu and Alo would be if they had grown up in this place?"

"They would probably be bad-tempered, like so many of these people," said Per.

48

Now the young anthropologist had the answer to her old question. "Much of what we are as adults is the result of where and how we grew up," Margaret said.

And because Margaret understood this, she never criticized the people of Manus for behaving as they did.

Margaret Mead knew that you cannot blame people for being different. If people have had different experiences, certainly they will be different. If you want to understand people, you must first understand how they live, which is often quite unlike the way you live.

Although the people of Manus were resentful and angry and unhappy, they knew that Margaret was a very special person. She listened to those who spoke to her, and she respected every member of the tribe. She understood them and accepted them just the way they were, so they loved her.

When Margaret left Manus at last, the people beat their drums with a sad, loud beat. It was a great tribute to her, and it was with sorrow that this wise and understanding woman was leaving them.

"Come back soon, Miss Markrit!" they called. "Come and see us again!"

In the years that followed her visit to Manus, Margaret Mead continued to travel in the South Seas. She lived with eight different primitive tribes and studied their ways. Some of them have names that sound strange to us. There were the Samoans, the Manus, and the Balinese. There were also the Arapesh, Mundugumor, Tchambuli, and Iatmul.

As she lived among these people, Mead learned to speak the language of each tribe she stayed with. She never forgot to listen, to watch, to pay attention. And she always tried to understand.

"All of these people have been my teachers," she said to Per Sun. "Each one has added to my understanding."

53

As she grew older, Margaret decided that understanding other
people had helped her to understand herself. "I am the way I am
partly because of where I grew up, and how I grew up," she said.

"That's true," said Per Sun. "When you were small you heard
your parents talk about learning and about trying to understand
other people. And you saw both of them studying and writing."

Margaret nodded. "It's only natural that I might want to do something similar."

And Margaret went on with her work very happily. She wrote twenty-four books by herself, and eighteen more with other people.

Margaret had been working and studying and writing for almost twenty-five years when she heard a very interesting piece of news.

What do you suppose it was?

She heard that the people who lived on the island of Manus—those people who had once been so angry—were now happier. "How wonderful!" said Margaret. "I must go to see this for myself."

Of course, Margaret always took her own thoughts with her, so Per Sun returned to Manus, too.

"They *do* seem happy," said Per Sun, after they landed and had a chance to look around.

The people of Manus saw their old friend Margaret then, and they rushed up to hug her. The children she had known were all grown up, and they talked and laughed with her.

"But you're so different!" said Margaret. "What has happened since I left here so long ago?"

"There was a war in this area," said one man, "and the American soldiers landed here. We taught them how to live on our island. In return, they told us much about America. We saw that some of the things we were doing were making us unhappy. We decided that we would treat our children differently."

"We learned much from the Americans," said a woman of Manus.

"And we have learned much from you," Margaret told them. "Indeed, people all over the world have learned from you."

"When I first came here many years ago, I hoped that I could understand you, and that I could help others to understand you. I believed that with this understanding, we would all know ourselves better. My hopes became realities. Today, many people know about Manus, and this knowledge has helped them to see why they are the way they are."

When it was time for Margaret to leave Manus again, the people hugged her once more and said a fond goodbye to their dear "Miss Markrit."

Margaret Mead continued to travel all over the world, but she never forgot the people of the South Seas who had taught her so much. She kept trying to learn more and understand more, and she shared what she learned when she spoke to large groups of people. She talked of many things—women's rights and child rearing and pollution and the energy crisis.

When Margaret Mead was more than seventy years old, people still flocked to hear her, and everyone marveled at *her* energy.

She seemed to be everywhere. She could be seen on the streets of New York, swinging her walking stick as she hurried to some important meeting. She was interviewed on the radio and she appeared on television. She wrote articles for magazines. Almost everyone wanted to spend time with her, or to read how she felt about important questions of the day.

Now you may not want to go off to some primitive island to try to understand people. You might just enjoy learning how to see things from another person's point of view right here at home. Perhaps when you understand someone else's point of view, both you and that other person will feel happier.

Just like our understanding friend Margaret Mead.

The End

Margaret Mead was born on December 16, 1901, in Philadelphia, Pennsylvania. Her father, Edward Sherwood Mead, was a professor of economics, and her mother, Emily Fogg Mead, was a social scientist. Her father's mother, Martha Ramsay Mead, a pioneer child psychologist, made her home with Margaret's family, so Margaret grew up in an environment that encouraged her to be intellectually alert and aware.

Margaret attended DePauw University in Indiana for one year, and then went to Barnard College in New York. Later she earned a Ph.D. in anthropology from Columbia University.

Margaret Mead pioneered a new approach to research in anthropology—going into the field to study the primitive societies of the world in order to understand more about people. Her first field expedition was in the island of Tau in the Samoan group, where she studied the development of adolescent girls under primitive conditions. Upon her return to the United States in 1926, Mead was appointed assistant curator of ethnology at the American Museum of Natural History in New York. Her association with the American Museum was to continue for the rest of her life.

Mead's best-known book, *Coming of Age in Samoa*, was completed and published in 1928, before she left to begin studying the Manus tribe of the Admiralty Islands. After her field trips to Samoa and the Admiralties, she studied other peoples of the Pacific—the Arapesh, Mundugumor, Tchambuli, Balinese, and Iatmal. She lived among these people and came to speak their languages.

Mead was the sole author of twenty-four books, and the co-author or editor of another eighteen. She wrote scores of scientific papers, as well as contributing to popular magazines and presenting hundreds of lectures on a wide variety of subjects.

In 1974, when she was 72, Margaret Mead—a woman in a male-dominated discipline—was elected to head the American Association for the Advancement of Science. This was only one of the many national and international honors

MARGARET MEAD
(1901–1978)

bestowed on her. She had become perhaps the world's most famous anthropologist. However, she remained unaffected by her fame.

She remained forever loyal to her causes and her friends. She went on with her writing and her lecturing, and she worked almost every day in her office at the museum.

The museum once drew up a list of subjects in which Mead was a specialist. The list read: "Education and culture; relationship between character structure and social forms; personality and culture; cultural aspects of problems of nutrition; mental health; family life; ecology; ekistics; transnational relations; national character; cultural change; and cultural building." She also lectured on a wide range of nonscientific subjects, from atomic politics to feminism.

Margaret Mead was a wonderful example of the vitality and energy that people of any age can generate when they have a clear purpose in life. Her purpose was simply to understand more about people, and to use the knowledge she gained to help others. She once said, "Knowledge about mankind, sought in reverence for life, can bring life."

The ValueTale Series